WEB MARKETING

MAHINROOP PM

PRINTED AND PUBLISHED BY AMAZON

Price

Ebook:$6

Paperback: $13

Introduction

'Web Marketing Super Course' is a comprehensive guide on web marketing worth reading and readers will definitely enjoy this amazing book. The book 'Web Marketing Super Course' is practical and easy to understand. Both technical and non technical audiences can get immensely benefitted from this book, the creative brainchild of a maverick IT professional. List of topics covered in the book include introduction to web marketing, advantages of web marketing, affiliate marketing, content marketing and web marketing best practices.

About the Author

MAHINROOP PM is an Information Technology Consultant based in India. He has published three books entitled as 'Mega Book of Website Designing', 'Blogging Masterclass Package 2018', and 'Big Book of Vatakara' respectively.

Written by MAHINROOP PM

Table of Contents

Introduction to Web Marketing

Web marketing is the process of using the web (internet) to market business and it includes the usage of social media, blogging and videos. There are huge opportunities for web marketing and banner ads, email promotions, and social media posting are the popular forms of web marketing. According to prominent web marketing professionals, web marketing offers unique benefits that other traditional marketing methods can't offer. Web marketing is a cost effective marketing method and it builds relationships with customers. New pricing, additional products and time sensitive sales can be handled with web marketing initiatives.

Web marketing is measurable and determining the Return on Investment of web marketing is very easy. Ability to quantify results is the best feature of web marketing initiatives and it will bring growth to an online/offline business. Businesses can build deeper connections with customers using web marketing and business owners can set their company apart if web marketing is effectively utilized. Web marketing helps a business to reach large number of buyers and digital marketing reaches worldwide. Internet marketing can energize the efforts of current marketing strategy and email marketing, social media marketing, content marketing, search engine optimization, Google ads, display ads and retargeting are the key types of web marketing.

Email marketing is one of the most frequently used types of web marketing and it is incredibly inexpensive. It has been pointed out that email marketing generates $38 in Return on Investment for every $1 spent. Social media marketing is inexpensive just like email marketing and getting into social media marketing is very simple. Content marketing has rocketed into prominence as an effective web marketing tool and the adage 'content is king' is familiar to everyone. Online advertisers find content marketing highly effective for their businesses and it is important to have a steady stream of high quality content.

Implementing search engine optimization helps content to get indexed in search engines organically. Effective search engine optimization brings more traffic to website and increases the chances of capturing more sales. Every business of contemporary age needs search engine optimization and SEO (Search Engine Optimization) traffic is more likely to convert. Google Ads are an integral part of web marketing because it places the business in front of huge audience. It has been reported that the Google ads are cost effective and businesses will need to pay only for click through. Display ads are a very successful web marketing method and its prices vary depending on the size and placement of the advertisement.

Retargeting is a prominent type of web marketing and it is absolutely essential in reengaging potential customers. It is a very well known fact that the term web marketing/internet marketing is multifaceted and in-depth. The different objectives of web marketing are growing website traffic, increasing social media followers, and expanding email database. It is quite important to setup a goal for web marketing and understanding the buyer is crucial to web marketing strategy. The ultimate decision on the type of web marketing depends on specific company and its business goals.

The branding message should be consistent in order to get benefitted from web marketing and the ability to directly measure Return on Investment is the marvellous feature of web marketing. Customers, prospects and partners are the lifeblood of web marketing of the contemporary era. Web marketing strategy can be positioned into a sustainable return on investment positive revenue engine. The web marketing can be used to make a solid revenue stream and it is to be kept in mind that content marketing is not just blogging. Content including articles, guides, webinars, eBooks, and videos are considered as powerful growth drivers for business. An ideal web marketing channel should be cost effective at acquiring customers and marketing automation, content management system and LinkedIn ads are powerful web marketing tools.

The list of leading web marketing tools includes Google Ads, social media, Google trends, Hub Spot, Buffer, Canva and Hootsuite. Search Engine Optimization is just one type of web marketing and web marketing provides sellers with accurate and real time results. The cost of web marketing is less when compared with traditional marketing and search engine marketing is a web marketing strategy that enhances website visibility on search engine results pages. Social media marketing is the process of promoting brands using social media channels like Facebook, YouTube, Instagram and Twitter. Blog posts, long form copy, eBooks, GIFs and info graphics are the leading channels of content marketing.

Pay per Click is a method of driving traffic to the website by Google Ad Words and Google Ad Words is the most common Pay per Click program. Affiliate marketing refers to the process of earning commission based on promoting other products or services. SMS marketing is a form of web marketing which uses short messaging service to reach the customers. Web marketing is highly beneficial for every business regardless of size and industry and B2B organizations will get hugely benefitted from web marketing. There are lots of job opportunities for web marketers as SEO managers, SEM specialists, PPC managers, affiliate marketers and content marketers.

Web marketing is unquestionably the most inexpensive way to reach target market and it drives traffic, leads and sales. The term web marketing is used interchangeably with content marketing and content marketing is the web marketing of today and future. Content marketing can be defined as the process of distributing valuable, relevant and consistent content. The content marketing is in direct opposition to traditional advertising and web marketing has showed tremendous success over the years. It has been estimated that content marketing will be an industry worth $313 billion by the year 2019.

Many business organizations all over the globe have adopted content marketing as an essential marketing tactic. According to the information available from web marketing industry, content marketing costs 62 percent less than traditional marketing. Blog posts and articles are one of the most common types of content marketing and blog has been recognized as a great content platform. Infographics is a content marketing method to present valuable information and podcast is the most prominent type of content marketing. Videos continue to be the hottest type of content and it is expected that videos will grab 82 percent of the internet traffic by 2021. Over 500 million hours of video is consumed on YouTube each and every single day and it depicts the power of video marketing.

Advantages of Web Marketing

Web marketing has become more popular as time passes by and it has eventually become the leading medium for marketing. The web marketing helps a business organization to nurture relationship with their customers. Personal and cost effective communication is the unique selling proposition of web marketing. Developing a professional web marketing campaign can attract more customers and convenience is the first and foremost advantage of web marketing. Web marketing has made downloading digital products from the internet possible with just few mouse clicks.

The web marketing offers better and comfortable online shopping experience to the customer of today. Low operating cost is another major advantage of web marketing and web marketing is cheaper when compared with traditional forms of marketing. The ability to measure and track results is another favourable feature of web marketing and the progress of web marketing campaign can be recorded. Web marketing features the ability to target audience based on demography and the ability to market products globally is another glorious advantage of web marketing. Aggressive Search Engine Optimization will help web marketing initiatives to reach millions of customers. The ability to multitask is another illustrious feature of web marketing and high adaptability is another renowned feature of web marketing.

Web marketing runs around the clock and the web marketing features automated as well as tech savvy marketing. Diversified marketing and advertising options make web marketing highly popular among small and medium sized businesses. Instant transaction service offered by web marketing companies makes it stand out from other traditional marketing methods. The instant transaction service has been made possible by third party payment processing companies like PayPal. Web marketing offers better sales relationships and marketers can easily collect email addresses of buyers in web marketing.

Web marketing is easy to start and quick to implement and a web marketing campaign can be created very effortlessly. Marketing campaign is one of the best advantages of web marketing and it has viral as well as long term effects. Web marketing methods like email marketing, social media marketing, search engine optimization, and Pay per Click offer multitude of benefits. Web marketing is all inclusive and both small and medium businesses can reap the benefits of web marketing. Internet marketing has become a modern day business tool and it enhances client base and marketing reach. Linked In has become the number one choice for professionally relevant content and wide range of potential customers, better response rate, long time exposure, better trust and increased brand awareness are the primary advantages of web marketing.

The first major benefit of web marketing is the capacity to highlight brand beyond local area and businesses are accessible to millions of clients with web marketing. One of the key attractions of web marketing is the capacity to handle large number of clients and continuity is another quintessential benefit of web marketing. Better brand management with 24/7 brand optimization is another impeccable feature of web marketing. Internet marketing is time effective and less or no start-up capital is required to channelize a successful web marketing campaign. An optimized web marketing campaign can ensure long term successful results and email marketing is one of the best web marketing procedures.

Everything can be automated in digital marketing and tools like Google Analytics can be used to measure the success of web marketing campaigns. Time saving opportunity is another key benefit of web marketing and web marketing ensures quick service delivery. A typical web marketing campaign can be optimized for the target audience and measurable Return on Investment, competitive advantage, niche product advantage, and specific customer targeting are the key features of web marketing. Internet marketing analytics tools can be used to test conversion rates and it showcases ad targeting based on gender, age, location and interests. Web marketing is rated as best in terms of personalization, transaction execution, and data collection.

Web marketing is an elegant combination of different strategies and it includes strategies like website design, search engine optimization and link building. The web marketing allows businesses such as online magazines and newspapers to deliver products to customers without using traditional mailing methods. Web marketing depicts low cost personalized communication and the barriers of business can be overcome with web marketing. Internet marketing allows personalizing customer offers and the web offers a key platform for building relationships with customers. Web marketing takes advantage of the growing importance of social media and social networking tools are incorporated in successful web marketing campaigns.

Consumers of today are turning on to the internet for buying decisions and digital marketing is more important than ever before. Mobile internet and social media are leading channels for web marketing in the contemporary era marked with explosive growth of internet. Businesses can easily make relationships with customers and clients with the help of internet marketing. Property maintenance costs and rental are not at all relevant to the internet marketing, the bandwagon of change in marketing. Web marketing allows convenient store hours and ecommerce store can be browsed on a 24/7 basis. According to top rated internet marketing professionals, web marketing provides a customized advertising approach.

Web marketing is a great tool to take advantage of social media channels including Facebook, Twitter, Pinterest and Instagram. Internet marketing provides an excellent way to build solid relationships with customers and web marketing helps in reaching more customers. Web marketing has scaled new heights of popularity in the recent years thanks to the internet and mobile revolution. Professional services make use of web marketing for building relationships, networking and lead generation. The huge growth of LinkedIn can be cited as the best example of the success saga of web marketing.

It has been pointed out that web marketing is really a very complex ecosystem of marketing techniques. Web marketing helps a business organization to build credibility and greater visibility within a very short time span. Online marketing offers many ways to build expertise and the internet is the most powerful marketing platform. It is possible to reach wide audience with the help of online marketing and blogging, social media and webinar have the capacity to reach millions of people. Web marketing can be used to establish relationships more effectively and LinkedIn groups can be used to converse with industry leaders. A business can target specific verticals or niches with the help of web marketing and web marketing is not tied to geography or time zone.

Affiliate Marketing

Affiliate marketing refers to earning commission by promoting the products of other people or companies. Merchant, network, publisher and customer are the four parties involved in the process of affiliate marketing. According to internet marketing maestros, affiliate marketing is the process of spreading product creation and product marketing. Solo entrepreneurs, start ups and multinational corporations could be the merchant behind an affiliate marketing program. Affiliates can range from single individuals to big companies and an affiliate promotes one or more affiliate products. A network acts as the intermediary between the affiliate and merchant in an affiliate marketing program.

Amazon, Click Bank, Commission Junction and JV Zoo offer some of the best affiliate marketing programs. The affiliate marketing program of Amazon is known as Amazon Associates and it is one of the most successful affiliate marketing programs. Affiliate marketing helps to turn product recommendations into passive income and it is an excellent alternate stream of income. The affiliate marketing is undoubtedly a lucrative revenue stream and it is an online sales tactic. Affiliate marketing lets affiliates to make money without creating products on their own and the performance based affiliate marketing is an integral part of business.

Steps involved in affiliate marketing

Find and join an affiliate program

Choose the offers to promote

Get unique affiliate link for each offer

Share links on blogs, social media platforms and website

Collect a commission when someone makes a purchase through the link

Affiliate commission rates vary depending on the company and offers and Click Bank is a premium internet retailer which offers top rated affiliate marketing program. There are some affiliate marketing programs that offer flat rate per sale and affiliate marketing offers numerous benefits to affiliates. There is no cost to join affiliate marketing programs and affiliates can make money with an established affiliate marketing company without any upfront investment. It has been reported that affiliate marketing is low risk and it continues to deliver steady pay cheques. It is to be kept in mind that great affiliate marketing is built on trust and some of the most popular affiliate platforms include Affiliate Network, Flex Offers, Share A Sale and Revenue Wire.

Shopify affiliate program is quite famous and affiliate marketing programs will have terms of service affiliates need to follow. A food blogger can promote the affiliate products of cookware, gourmet ingredients, as well as meal kits. According to ace internet marketers, affiliate marketing revenue will eventually become a form of passive income. The success in affiliate marketing is largely dependent upon the overall size of the following and internet marketers promote affiliate marketing programs by offering bonuses to anyone who purchase the order. Some affiliate marketers offer a free eBook to any follower who made a purchase and Wirecutter and Buzzfeed are the examples of businesses using affiliate marketing.

According to a recent statistics, 81% of brands and 84% of publishers leverage the power of affiliate marketing. There is a 10.1% increase in affiliate marketing spending in the United States of America every year. The affiliate can be an individual or company that markets the seller's products in an appealing way to potential customers. Affiliates will often have a specific audience to whom they market and they are paid by pay per sale, pay per lead and pay per click. Pay per Sale is the standard affiliate marketing structure and the pay per lead is a more complex system in affiliate marketing.

The pay per lead compensates affiliates based on the conversion of leads and the affiliate is paid based on the increase in web traffic in the pay per click model. Affiliate marketing is a very large industry and it has become a key income source for numerous bloggers all over the globe. More and more business organizations are getting involved in affiliate marketing and it is an excellent passive income stream. AWIN is one of the best affiliate networks in the world and it is a very comprehensive affiliate network. According to the information available from the market, AWIN works with both digital and physical products.

The commission rates in AWIN depend upon the campaign and the merchant or advertiser and AWIN is the best option for experienced affiliates. AWIN showcases lots of powerful tools like opportunity marketplace, WordPress plug-in and Google Chrome extension. Click Bank has been around in the affiliate marketing field since the early days of internet and it focuses on digital products. Few affiliate programs are bigger than Click Bank and it offers both physical as well as digital products today. The main focus of Click Bank is on ebooks, online courses and ecourses as an affiliate network.

The commission rate of Click Bank is up to a whopping 75% and Click Bank allows affiliate markets to join for free. The approval process of Click Bank is virtually automatic and it is recommended for marketers entering the affiliate marketing arena for the first time. Weekly payouts with different payout options are another excellent feature of Click Bank and its joint venture program allows marketers to gain higher returns. Click Bank has streamlined innovation in the affiliate marketing arena as one of the biggest and most robust affiliate marketing programs. Shopify is a very popular option for building ecommerce stores and its affiliate program pays commissions on all referred purchases of Shopify products and services.

Content Marketing

Content marketing is a marketing approach focused on creating and distributing valuable content to drive customer action. Leading brands use content marketing and majority of marketers in the contemporary era make use of content marketing. Multinational corporations, medium sized businesses, one person shops, and solo entrepreneurs get benefitted from content marketing. Increased savings, cost savings and better loyal customers are the key reasons for adopting content marketing. According to ace digital marketing strategists, content is unquestionably the present and future of marketing.

It is a fact that marketing is impossible without great content and quality content contains all forms of marketing including social media marketing, search engine optimization, press releases, Pay per Click, and inbound marketing. Content marketing strategy is equally important just like social media strategy and search engines reward businesses that provide quality content. Content is key to driving inbound traffic and blogs, Twitter, Facebook and viral YouTube videos are the most popular forms of content marketing. Content marketing has been around ever since the inception of internet and content marketing is all about storytelling. The content marketing is a long term strategy that focuses on building a strong relationship with target audiences. Content marketing shows that a business actually cares about its customers and the very basic foundation of content marketing is high quality content.

Content marketing is all about information and the ultimate objective of content marketing is to attract customers by creating valuable content. Effective content marketing will create a very big impact and content marketing can be used to promote a brand. The purpose of content marketing is to attract more qualified leads and nurture customer relationships. It has been found that content marketing and inbound marketing are often used interchangeably. According to street smart internet marketers, content marketing is a subset of inbound marketing.

Content marketing refers to the act of sharing content in a consumable format including blog articles, videos, podcasts, social media marketing, webinars and Infographics. The content marketing focuses on broad target audience and blogging is the foundation of content marketing. Extensive amount of information can be shared through ebooks and videos are more engaging to the buyer persona. Content marketing taps into the awareness and research stages of the buying process and the return on investment for content marketing is absolutely phenomenal. High quality content marketing contributes to SEO (Search Engine Optimization) marketing efforts. The impact of content marketing on the SEO power of a website is very huge and there is no such thing as SEO without content. Internet marketers are aware of the fact that 'content is king' and keyword research is essential for successful content marketing.

Content marketing has gained thumping victory as a marketing method and producing great content is the easy way to get more back links. The content marketing initiatives improve customer service and content marketing has huge importance in public relations. It is a well known fact that blog posts have replaced press releases in the contemporary age and Facebook live has replaced press conferences. Content marketing has eventually become an industry standard and it is essential to build a brand in 2019 and beyond. The content marketing gives businesses a big advantage in the contemporary age and content marketing is effective as an inbound marketing campaign.

Blogging is the fastest way of content marketing and it is essential to blog as frequently as possible. Sharing content through social media outlets will maximize the potential of individual blog posts. Content marketing is beneficial for both B2B (Business to Business) and B2C (Business to Consumer) marketers. It is quite important to provide content worth reading and content marketing is used by 86% of businesses today. Effective content marketing harnesses the power of best copywriting and content marketing and copywriting can be combined to get amazing results. Content marketing is one of the most integral parts of web marketing campaigns of today and there is valuable content behind every brand.

High quality content connects a brand with audience and content marketing improves brand reputation to a very great extent. Ideal content in a website of the contemporary age is educational, engaging, valuable as well as entertaining. Publishing content through third party publishers and sharing content with influencers will help a business to build trust within the target market. Great content is highly helpful in influencer conversions and effective content marketing improves website conversions. The conversion rates of content marketing are higher than the conversion rates of other web marketing methods.

Content marketing increases the market leads of a company and video content provides great Return on Investment. Clear call to action is the inseparable element of effective content marketing and high quality content affects search engine optimization. Content creation is the most effective SEO technique and content marketing has been recognized as a cost effective way to bring in new leads. Content marketing is an affordable method for lead generation and it provides rich dividends to small businesses. The whole process of content marketing is time intensive and it will take some time to see the results of content marketing efforts. Content marketing provides huge return on investment that small businesses can't ignore and it produces three times as many leads as paid search advertisements.

An ideal content marketing strategy should take target market into consideration and content enables a brand to showcase subject matter expertise. A business can publish great content if they want to build relationships with their customers and content is a key part of building trust. Content marketing is important mainly because leads as well as customers want great content. The content marketing helps a business organization to stand out from the rest and it shows what makes a company special. Content is important during each step of the marketing funnel and it supports every other marketing strategy.

Businesses need to create consistent and quality content and content marketing integrates all other forms of web marketing. A well crafted content marketing strategy helps a business organization to scale heights of excellence. Content marketing lets marketers to become publishers by building their own audiences and attracting customers. Content is closely tied to the buying journey of a customer and creating personalized content is absolutely important. The content should be suitable for each stage of buyer's journey and content marketing is a completely unique approach. Internet marketing experts unanimously agree that content marketing is a great way to build organic awareness. It is a very well known fact that valuable content ranks highly on search engines like Google, Yahoo and Bing.

Importance of Web Marketing

Businesses of contemporary era understood the importance of web marketing and web marketing is highly effective as a marketing strategy. Web marketing helps a company to grow business and it is important because customers of today are online. Internet marketing helps businesses to connect with leads that are interested in business and it creates two way communication. The importance of web marketing lies in its ability to create two way communication and businesses can reach customers through different marketing channels. Digital marketing helps businesses to communicate better with audience and it personalizes the experience of audience.

Effective web marketing creates a customized experience for every member in the audience and businesses can create tailored experience using internet marketing. Internet marketing is popular because of its ability to create personalized marketing strategy and web marketing paves the way towards qualified traffic. Web marketing allows businesses to target by demographics, hobbies, interests as well as spending habits. Digital marketing increases the visibility of a business and the business is exposed to billions of people on the internet. An internet business is visible to audience on a 24/7 basis and content marketing, social media marketing and video marketing can be used to increase the visibility of a business.

The capability to run multiple campaigns is another illustrious feature of web marketing and web marketing is a cost effective strategy for business. The internet marketing drives quality return on investment and web marketing methods are relatively affordable when compared to other marketing methods. Web marketing campaigns can be created very fast and the analytics of every marketing campaign can be easily measured. Click through rate, impressions, views and reactions are the most common metrics in web marketing analytics. Internet marketing is a valuable way for businesses to grow and the web marketing plays a key role in business success.

Internet marketing has become an essentiality to promote products as well as services and brand visibility, increased traffic and increased sales are the key benefits of web marketing. Web marketing is beneficial for all types of businesses and connecting with customers is the preliminary objective of web marketing. Internet marketing has become a crucial component of businesses of today and digital marketing helps a business to grow and thrive. Social media marketing and advertising are only one component of web marketing of the contemporary age. Web marketing is really a beacon of hope for small businesses and brick and mortar stores, ecommerce stores and personal brands are the key beneficiaries of web marketing.

Web marketing allows small businesses to compete with a very small budget and the ability to dissect huge demographics is the colourful specialty of web marketing. Google Ad Words is the classic example of search advertising campaign and Pay per Click campaigns allow businesses to position near the top of searches. According to fabled internet marketers, web marketing is equipped with the power of segmentation, automation and personalization. Working with a web marketing company offers infinite benefits to a typical business and web marketing is easy to scale. Email marketing has the highest return on investment and the email marketing software is a conversion machine.

Combination of social media marketing and content marketing offers innumerable benefits for an internet marketing company. Content marketing can generate more leads than traditional marketing and web marketing integrates marketing with mobile technology. Web marketing has fundamentally changed every aspect of our lives and it refers to a very broad category of advertising. Most of the online advertising spaces are free to use and paid search marketing costs only a fraction of a typical television advertising campaign. Innovative examples of web marketing include Absolut, Sony, Axe, Burger King and Sixt. Web marketing features wide range of marketing strategies and social media marketing manager, digital marketer and SEO specialist are the shining careers in web marketing.

Social media marketing managers direct marketing campaigns using Facebook, Twitter, YouTube and other marketing channels. Web marketing is the best way to reach out more targeted customers and it provides something innovative to the consumer too. The digital modes of marketing are easily customizable and the conversion rate of web marketing is higher. Marketing automation, content marketing, big data, mobile marketing, social media marketing, conversion rate optimization, search engine optimization and online PR are the web marketing activities with greatest impact in 2019. Web marketing offers multiple ways to interact with customers and digital marketing generates 2.8 times more revenue.

Internet marketing has become more important than ever and it has become essential for business success in the contemporary era. Web marketing has huge role in modern day marketing and it is beneficial to every aspect of the business. The web marketing has redefined the relationship between businesses to businesses and businesses to consumers. Web marketing helps organizations to obtain better global branding and an internet marketing campaign can be easily tracked, measured and tested. Having the right web marketing strategies is essential to succeed in the contemporary digital business landscape. Web marketing increases the visibility of an organization and it enables more direct detailed market research.

Web marketing has the capacity to successfully engage customer base and product awareness is one of the key reasons for launching a web marketing campaign. Online marketing enhances sales and web marketing increases the credibility of a particular business. According to humdinger web marketing experts, successful web marketing translates to increased traffic. Time variations in different parts of the globe won't affect web marketing and businesses can avoid the high cost of marketing by implementing web marketing. Internet marketing is cheaper than radio and television advertisements and social network tools can be easily integrated in a web marketing campaign.

Businesses can personalize communication between them and their clients using web marketing. An effective web marketing strategy helps a business organization to stand out from the rest and the objectives of web marketing campaign should be very clearly established. The key objective of an internet marketing campaign is search engine friendliness and a web marketing strategy should be chalked out keeping in mind the products and services. An ideal web marketing strategy will have a clear cut objective and a web marketing campaign should be as simple as possible. High performance and large coverage of target audience are the principal benefits of web marketing.

Web Marketing Job Responsibilities

Web marketing jobs include web marketing consultant, SEO consultants, content marketer, and search engine marketing specialist. The web marketing depicts the kaleidoscope of colourful career and web marketing professionals are known for instinctual web marketing skills. Most of the web marketing professionals are graduated in marketing, English, business, journalism, and communication. A conventional web marketing expert is a creative problem solver and an excellent communicator. Degree program for web marketing consists of courses in web design, writing, multimedia and media marketing.

Excellent organizational skills and proficiency in web programming are the key skills possessed by web marketing professional. Web marketer will have comprehensive knowledge in search engine optimization, Pay per Click, blogging, social networking and email marketing. Web marketing executives oversee the digital marketing initiatives of their organization and they execute digital marketing campaigns. Digital marketers work for online retailers, financial institutions, publishers and charity organizations. Digital marketing agencies employ web marketing professionals and web marketing executive will manage digital marketing campaign and oversee social media strategy. Management and maintenance of the organization website is another key job responsibility of web marketing executive. Writing and optimizing content for website is another functionality of a typical web marketing professional. Conceptualizing attractive content for social media networks like Facebook and Twitter is another prime job responsibility of web marketer.

It is a well known fact that web marketers track and analyze traffic flow along with providing regular internal reports. Web marketers are assigned with the responsibility of search engine optimization of the website. Video editing, video posting, webinar creation, web series creation, online banner adverts creation, Pay per Click management and copywriting for email marketing campaign are the key job responsibilities of web marketing professional. Typical web marketers are polyhistor IT professionals and they are busy with future proofing innovative web marketing solutions. Web marketing professionals are passionate about identifying trends in web marketing and writing blog posts is an integral part of the job responsibilities of web marketer.

Video editing skills and web development skills punctuate a typical web marketing professional. A web marketing professional should have a comprehensive knowledge of HTML, JavaScript, Microsoft Word, Microsoft PowerPoint, and search engine optimization. Web marketing managers will have crystal clear idea of Google Ad Words, Pay per Click, Google Analytics, brand marketing, content marketing networks, analytical tools, and Facebook marketing. A typical web marketing professional will carry out YouTube marketing and Instagram marketing. YouTube marketing manager is entrusted with the responsibility of creating a big and successful YouTube channel. Web marketing is a dynamic and booming career avenue and the creation of innovative digital marketing strategies is the first responsibility of a web marketing professional.

Digital marketing is unquestionably an excellent career option and it features a glimmering career path. The career of web marketing is for innovative and creative professionals equipped with inquisitiveness. Web marketing is a highly results driven job and it enhances knowledge as well as creative skills. Web marketers maintain and supply content for a business organization website and they are skilled in creating SMS and email based marketing campaigns. The job responsibility of a digital marketing manager is to develop, implement and manage marketing campaign.

Enhancing brand awareness, driving website traffic and acquiring leads are the key job responsibilities of web marketing manager. The primary role of a Search Engine Optimization specialist is to rank website page on the search engine results page. The job of SEO executive will be always in high demand and SEO executives are employed by large companies with marketing departments. High level of technical skill is needed to become a rock star web marketing professional today. On page SEO, off page SEO, link building, performance analysis, and keyword research are the duties of SEO executive. Social media marketing expert is another shining career in the web marketing world and the social media marketing manager combines marketing and social media management.

Interaction with target audience, content promotion and expanding the opportunities for increasing the revenue are the main job responsibilities of web marketing professional. A social media marketing manager should have knowledge of social media channels, social media marketing, and content optimization. Social media marketing expert is engaged in promoting the brand's products on various social media channels. A web marketing copywriter produces the written content for web pages and they work as either freelance copywriter or employee of the company. A web copywriter should understand the interests of target audience and copywriter writes for blogs, web pages, social media, ebooks, and video script.

Digital marketing manager performs the jobs of search engine marketer in small companies and there will be a separate SEM specialist in big companies. Bid management, keyword research, and advertisement copywriting are the job duties of Search Engine Marketing Specialist. Search engine marketing specialists try their level best to achieve maximum return on investment in paid search campaigns. The inbound marketing manager is responsible for attracting traffic and qualified prospects. He/she manages rich content like blog posts, ebooks, webinars, whitepapers, Infographics and reports. An inbound marketing manager optimizes marketing automation through social media channels, content channels and email.

The content marketing manager is responsible for content marketing and blog management, marketing campaign management, ebook publishing, guest blogging, email communication and video marketing are the chief job responsibilities of content marketing manager. A content marketing manager in a web marketing company is a master expert in creating, editing and improving the content. The content marketing manager should have excellent understanding of SEO best practices and content development. Web analytics manager is responsible for the implementation of tools and strategies in web marketing.

Job Responsibilities of Analytics Manager

Understand the business objectives

Develop the right strategies for data analysis

Configure analytical solutions

The digital marketing career is evolving as time passes by and it is a lucrative career segment for self styled IT professionals. Digital marketing features immense career opportunities and fondness for new technology characterises a web marketing professional. The duties of web marketing managers include planning campaigns, analyzing metrics and identifying trends. Digital marketing managers are skilled in social media and the ideal web marketing professional will have experience in marketing as well as social media management. A web marketing professional/SEO executive/content marketer exhibits excellent analytical and interpersonal skills. Developing and monitoring campaign budgets are another important responsibility of web marketing executives. They are experts in generating reports of internet marketing campaigns and web marketing manager works along with media experts to improve marketing results.

Search Engine Optimization

Search Engine Optimization is the process of getting organic traffic from search engines like Google, Yahoo and Bing. It is a very well known fact that on page SEO and off Page SEO are two types of SEO (Search Engine Optimization). SEO factors work in combination and no single SEO factor will guarantee search engine results. High quality website content is the most important factor as far as Search Engine Optimization is concerned. Search engine algorithms change frequently and SEO tactics evolve according to the search engine algorithm changes.

Search engine optimization is a collection of strategies, techniques and tactics to get higher search engine rankings. SEO is about making search engine results relevant to the user's search query and search engine optimization is valuable and important. Effective Search Engine Optimization strategies deliver more traffic, sales, revenue, profit and leads. Search engine optimization is important for the success of any online business and SEO is a great way to increase the quality of a website. SEO marketing is more important than ever today and good SEO practices improve the user experience. SEO is good for the social promotion of the website and Search Engine Optimization is important for the smooth running of a website.

Search engine algorithms take number of factors into account and optimizing website for search engines will give an advantage over non optimized websites. Search engine optimization is a framework with rules and technical SEO ensures that search engines can crawl the website without any issues. The first step in SEO process is called as the technical SEO and on page SEO deals with content as well as site structure. On page SEO consists of website structure, SEO keywords, title optimization, headings, internal links, image optimization, and structured data mark up. It has been pointed out that on page SEO will improve the usability and credibility of a website or blog.

Content optimization is part of on page SEO and link building is the key off page SEO technique. Typical on page SEO plan include meta tags, image optimization, content optimization, sitemap indexing, broken links checking, website folder structure, RSS feed creation, and Robots.txt. Off page SEO plan includes search engine submissions, general directory submissions, product based directory submissions, article submission, press release submission, RSS feed promotion and video uploading. Good content in a website will pave the way towards natural links and SEO is one of the tools available in web marketing arsenal. Good content is the most important success factor of SEO and it is difficult to optimize a website without quality content.

Search engine optimization will give the website an extra boost and it revolves around Google today. SEO is definitely a cost effective web marketing technique and real SEO is a little bit challenging. Success in search engine optimization is dependent upon understanding the most important SEO ranking factors.

Advantages of SEO for marketing

Highly targeted

Low cost visitors

Dynamic

Search engine marketing is only one digital communication tool and SEO can be done by making some simple tweaks to website content. Search engine optimization is one of the cheapest and easiest ways to drive more traffic to the website. A search engine works by crawling, indexing and querying and it runs a program called spider to find content on the web. The content in a website should be high quality and informative to get indexed in prominent search engines. Content that impresses a human being will most probably impress the search engine giant Google too. 2500+ words articles and blog posts get indexed well in search engines including the one and only Google. Well researched content gets indexed well in Google and it is important to update the website with fresh content. Keywords are still an important element of SEO strategy and Google Keyword Planner is the best tool for finding the keywords.

The title tag should essentially display an accurate description of the content on the page and it is critical to SEO. Title tag should be kept between 50-60 characters and it should accurately describe content on the page. Links can provide great value in terms of SEO and internal links and external links are the two types of links. Internal link connects one page of website to another and external link directs the user to an outside domain. SEO is an essential part of any web marketing strategy of today and it can help a business to build brand.

It is a fact that an optimized website earns more traffic and SEO boosts credibility and authority of a website. According to assertive internet marketing professionals, SEO efforts can be combined with content marketing. One of the biggest impacts of search engine optimization is that it is easy to measure and Google Analytics can be used to monitor traffic and referral sources. The ultimate objective of SEO is to improve ranking in search engines and a website should be optimized for the mobile first index. The rankings of a site that does not perform well on Smartphones and tablets will definitely suffer.

The list of most prominent keyword research tools includes Google Keyword Planner, Uber Suggest and Keyword.io. SEM Rush, Screaming frog, and redirect path are the best tools to improve on page search engine optimization. Ahrefs and Open Site Explorer are the recommended tools to improve off page optimization. Google Analytics and Google Search Console can be used to measure the impact of web marketing campaign. GT Metrix and Crazy Egg are the best tools to improve conversion rate of search engine optimization.

Planning and lots of patience are required to achieve results using search engine optimization methods. According to buggy internet marketing professionals, SEO is a great investment for ecommerce websites. It helps an ecommerce store to make sales on autopilot with no recurring expense and the best ecommerce SEO strategy includes keyword research, site architecture, on page SEO, technical SEO, local SEO, link building, and content marketing. Search engine optimization is the art and science of optimizing a website and SEO has a creative user experience aspect. Using better images, videos and examples is a key aspect of ecommerce Search Engine Optimization. Beautiful and eye catching photographs and glittering product descriptions characterize a typical ecommerce store. SEO is a holistic effort of social media, marketing, web designing, copywriting and networking.

Types of Web Marketing

The list of different types of web marketing include search engine optimization, search engine marketing, pay per click, content marketing, social media marketing, affiliate marketing, and email marketing. Search engine optimization is the process of getting organic traffic from search engines including the Google. Search Engine Marketing (SEM) refers to gaining website traffic by purchasing advertisements on search engines. Google Ad Words is the most popular paid search platform followed by Bing ads and content marketing is the process of creating and distributing valuable content. Quality content is the integral part of social media marketing, SEO, press releases, inbound marketing and content strategy.

Social media marketing helps a business organization to build brand equity, improve customer experience, and collect customer feedback. Affiliate marketing is the process of earning a commission by promoting other people's products. Email marketing provides direct contact with clients and it drives prospective customers to a website. Social media marketing is the process of acquiring sales through the use of social media platforms like Facebook, Twitter and Instagram. Organic social media marketing focuses on building a community and harnessing the power of customer relations is another key aspect of social media marketing. Immediately replying to the customers on social media channels add a level of authenticity and it inspires other people to trust products.

Social media marketing is closely interrelated with content marketing and social media is the best place to promote valuable content. Paid social media marketing is another major type of web marketing and Facebook Ads is a popular one. Each social media platform has its own suite of paid promotional options and a dedicated Facebook ad is tailored to marketing objectives. Search engine optimization maximises the number of visitors to a web page and on page SEO and off page SEO are two most common types of SEO. SEO is closely related to content marketing and the largest part of off page SEO is the generation of back links.

A great way to generate back links is by creating high quality content and the objective of content marketing is to convert target market into customers. Blog posts, videos, industry reports, Infographics, ebooks, podcasts, case studies and webinars are the leading forms of content marketing. Content marketing works closely with social media marketing and search engine optimization. Social media is one of the main channels used to distribute and promote content and influencer marketing is the process of working with influencers to promote a product or service. Influencer marketing was available only to larger brands before the advent of internet and everyone can engage in influencer marketing today.

Affiliate marketing is online referral marketing and it allows internet marketers to earn money by promoting product of another business. The well known website host and domain registrar Blue Host has a popular affiliate marketing program. Affiliate marketing is intertwined with social media marketing, content marketing and influencer marketing. The true power of email marketing is often underestimated and email marketing campaigns will start with lead magnet. Paid advertising is a type of web marketing in which advertisers show their ads on online platforms like Facebook, LinkedIn and YouTube.

Paid advertising is often referred as PPC (Pay per Click) and advertisers in a PPC campaign are charged per cost per thousand impressions, cost per view and cost per action. The biggest digital advertising platforms in the universe are Google and Facebook, the grace of blossoming IT landscape. Target audience can be defined in Facebook by demographics, interests, behaviours and more. Many forms of web marketing such as social media marketing, content marketing and SEO can be done for free. Most small businesses prefer web marketing because it is less expensive and different types of web marketing can be combined together. Good SEO practice makes the website more user friendly and email marketing is still considered as one of the main types of web marketing.

Email marketing can be used to give special discounts, exclusive content, personalized offers, and other special things. According to skilled digerati, PPC (Pay per Click) campaign and SEO campaign are built around keywords. Blog marketing has eventually become a very popular form of web marketing and it converts traffic into leads. YouTube has become a synonym for video marketing and it is the second largest search engine in the world now. Video marketing offers excellent return on investment compared with other forms of web marketing.

There are lots of free video editing tools available today and high quality video can made using the Smartphone. Web marketing is undoubtedly a powerful marketing tool and different types of web marketing are found to be effective. Search engine optimization makes use of website elements such as titles, keywords, image and menus. Low cost is the striking attraction of social media marketing and quick measurement of success is the benefit of Pay per Click. Different marketing channels like email, display advertisements, and paid search advertisements influence customers at different points in the path to purchase. SEO is the most important type of web marketing and it increases authority and Alexa scores. The whole search engine optimization process paves the way towards more traffic, activity as well as conversions.

The list of most popular SEO tools includes Moz SEO tools, Bing web master tools and Google Keyword planner. Guest blogging, direct mail, and collateral material are some of the best search engine optimization practices. Blog writing, content optimization and social media are the best organic Search Engine Optimization practices. According to web marketing masterminds, pay per click is one of the effective and fastest types of web marketing. Email marketing is termed as one of the best web marketing channels in terms of optimizing sales.

Video marketing acts as one of the most innovative types of web marketing and social media marketing is an inventive type of web marketing. Affiliate marketing can be called as a commissioned sales job and guest blogging and purchasing reviews from bloggers are examples of contextual marketing. Web marketing is a branch of marketing which is constantly evolving as well as changing and an internet marketer channelizes different types of marketing channels. Search engine optimization is one of the fastest growing types of web marketing and executing SEO intensifies marketing campaign. Businesses can use content marketing to share valuable information and display advertising refers to the use of web banners placed on third party websites or blogs.

Video Marketing

Every business of today needs a video marketing strategy and video is an integral part of overall web marketing plan. Video production has become more cost effective than ever and it is possible to shoot high quality 4K video with the Smartphone. Video marketing refers to the usage of video to promote and market a product or service in the contemporary business landscape. The objectives of video marketing are increasing engagement on social media channels and educating consumers. Recent years witnessed the popularity of video as a content marketing form and video marketing rose into prominence as a holistic business approach.

It is a fact that personalized video is shaping the future of marketing, sales as well as customer service. Video in landing page can increase the conversion rate by over 80% and videos help buyers to make an informed buying decision. Video marketing has transformed the market and it has revolutionized how sales people connect with prospects. Video is incredibly useful throughout the web marketing journey and it is a very versatile tool for sales professionals. On boarding videos, knowledge based videos, video calls, and customer story videos brought a new era of innovation in the web marketing arena. Video is within the reach of any business and most of the marketers of today add YouTube to their content strategy.

Demo videos, brand videos, event videos, educational videos, explainer videos, animated videos, customer testimonial videos, live videos, virtual reality videos and augmented reality videos are the key types of marketing videos. The demo videos showcase how a product works and brand videos are created as a part of advertising campaign. According to polymath web marketing professionals, the objective of brand video is to spread awareness about the company. Instructional videos can be used to teach the audience something new and they are equipped with effulgence of creativity. Educational and how to videos are used by sales as well as service teams of a business organization.

Explainer videos are mainly used to help the audience better understand why they need a typical product. Animated video is a great option for explaining complex concepts and customer testimonial videos are quite popular. Steps involved in video production include planning the video, scripting the video, using camera, setting up studio, organizing the footage, choosing music and recording the voice over. A strong web marketing campaign incorporates video and video is a goldmine for SEO (Search Engine Optimization). Video can increase search engine rankings, click through rates, open rates as well as conversions. YouTube is the second largest search engine and it is owned by the search engine tycoon Google.

There are countless platforms for video marketing including YouTube, Vimeo, broadcast television and video boards. Consumers all over the globe can access an online media anytime, anywhere with their laptop or Smartphone. The ability to reach millions of customers in a cost effective way is the key feature of video marketing. Well known internet marketers opine that video marketing is a very powerful platform since it combines visual and audio. Video marketing is highly effective as a marketing medium and it is a forward facing marketing strategy.

The video marketing is data driven and storytelling is a key part of video marketing of the contemporary age. The audience should be engaged with marketing videos and there is no set length for marketing videos. Videos distributed in social media channels will have a big effect and video metrics can be tracked. Video marketing is all over the internet and it is easily quantifiable by statistics. Everyone is aware of the fact that video helps to get back links to a website and it boosts likes as well as shares. Videos boost information retention and video content accounts for 74% of the online traffic. 63% of the business organizations have started using video content marketing and video marketing is a key part of web marketing strategy.

Having video content in the marketing campaign ensures that businesses are maximizing the outreach potential. Businesses can dominate the business landscape with amazing video content and video marketing will surely increase the sales and leads. A business can invest in video marketing if their objective is to increase brand awareness and connect with customers in an innovative way. Video is considered as an excellent tool to leverage the goals of a company and organic engagement on Facebook is higher if the post includes video. A major chunk of web marketers incorporate video into their marketing campaigns and companies who used video marketing have witnessed increase in click through rates and web conversion rates.

It has been estimated that online content will consist of eighty percent video marketing by 2019. Mobile consumption of video content rises by 100 percent annually and high quality videos are an absolute must have for websites, social media channels and digital platforms. Video marketing is the act of incorporating video into the marketing strategy of a company and customers of today are immersed in the world of video marketing. More marketers are switching on to video marketing mainly because of the innumerable benefits it offers. The primary benefits of video marketing include increased brand awareness, increased conversions, improved return on investment and customer trust.

Business organizations have reported increase in conversions on pages with videos and landing page is the best place to showcase videos. Video marketing has gained riveting achievement as a web marketing strategy and YouTube depicts the colourful aspects of video marketing. Ace web marketing experts agree that explainer videos provide lots of value to current as well as potential customers. Marketing professionals name video as the type of content with best Return on Investment in 2019. The goal of video marketing is to build trust within community of potential clients and existing customers.

Search engines including Google love videos and videos with optimized titles, descriptions and keywords perform better. Video marketing is a win-win marketing strategy and authentic storytelling through video will definitely increase engagement. The quality of videos is very important and it should be educative, entertaining, helpful, relevant and engaging. A company profile or branded video illustrates high level overview of the products and services a company offers. The objective of company profile video is to increase brand awareness and create more interest among the target audience. Company profile video is helpful in increasing sales conversions and it can be posted on the home page of company website.

Web Marketing and Social Media

Social media marketing is a powerful medium to reach prospects and customers and web marketing on social media will bring remarkable results. The social media marketing is a web marketing initiative that involves sharing content on social media sites in order to achieve branding goals. Social media marketing includes posting text, image updates, videos and paid social media advertising. The goals of business should be considered before chalking out a social media marketing campaign. An ecommerce or travel business can get immense value from social media channels like Instagram or Pinterest.

A business to business or a web marketing company can reap rich benefits through Twitter, Facebook or LinkedIn. The list of social media marketing goals include increasing web traffic, building conversions, increasing brand awareness, creating brand identity and improving communication with audiences. Building an effective social media marketing plan is essential in the contemporary age of intense business competition. It is important to create great social content like images, videos, Infographics, how to guides, blog posts and ebooks. A consistent brand image should be created through all leading social media channels including Facebook, Twitter, Pinterest, Instagram and LinkedIn. Social media is the best place for sharing high quality website and blog content with customers all over the world.

Great blog content will help a business to gain more followers in social media outlets and Google Analytics can be used as an excellent social media marketing tool. Different social media marketing channels require different approaches and it is necessary to develop a unique strategy for each platform. Facebook Business Fan Page is an excellent social media strategy and businesses should consider a cost effective Facebook ad strategy. The Facebook ad strategy will have a big impact on organic Facebook presence and the image centred platform of Pinterest is ideal for retail businesses. Pinterest allows businesses to showcase product offerings with eye catching pinboards and the primary audience of Pinterest is female.

Twitter is a top rated social media marketing tool and it revolves around dialogue and communication. LinkedIn is the social media marketing site for professionals and it is a great platform to share content with likeminded individuals. The LinkedIn is a fantastic tool for posting jobs and employee networking in the current internet age. YouTube is the number one social network for creating and sharing video content and it is an undisputable fact that YouTube is a very powerful social media marketing tool. The videos created by some businesses go viral and they may become a sensational hit in the cyber world.

Useful and interactive 'how to' videos are hugely popular in YouTube and YouTube marketing has huge SEO benefits too. Social media platforms like Yelp and Four Square are perfect for location based brick and mortar businesses. The high pitched social media initiatives like Reddit, Stumble Upon and Digg are ideal for sharing compelling content. Reddit has huge social media marketing potential with a whopping two billion page views a month. Social media marketing is something more than improving site traffic and helping businesses reach more customers.

Paid social advertising is a cost effective web marketing strategy and Facebook is one of the most powerful advertising platforms. Twitter is a social site that let people share short messages called as tweets and Facebook is a fully fledged social networking site that allows sharing updates and photos. Social media marketing is helpful in building quality back links and search engine optimization efforts. The social media is just one of the available channels of web marketing and social media is the latest buzzword in web marketing. The most popular social media marketing platforms are Facebook, Twitter, Pinterest, Instagram, Tumblr, LinkedIn, Stumble Upon and YouTube. Social media marketing is the fastest way to spread word about a marketing offer and the social media marketing is relevant from SEO perspective.

Social media marketing has eventually become a trend and it is one of the best ways to interact with customers. Social media is a major component of web marketing and it is limited to the boundaries of the internet. A web marketing campaign may include one or more component while social media marketing may include one or more social media platforms. Social media is closely interrelated with content strategy and social media marketing strategy depends on the brand, products and services. The success or failure of a social media marketing campaign depends on many factors like the experience of web marketing consultant.

Social media marketing is the future of web marketing and it has changed the way businesses promote products. A social media strategy should necessarily include the following.

Set actionable business goals

Research the audience

Establish most important metrics

Analyze competition

Create engaging content

Assess the results and optimize

Internet marketers should keep in mind that social media marketing is a marathon and the creation of authentic brand awareness is the ultimate objective of an ideal social media marketing plan. Brick and mortar businesses look for social media strategy that drives in-store sales and social media Return on Investment doesn't happen by accident. Creation of loyal fan base is the first and foremost objective of social media marketing and promoting user generated content is a vital part of social media strategy.

90% of internet marketers say that social media marketing has increased their business exposure and social media marketing plays a pivotal role in growing the brand. An active social media presence helps a business to build relationship with their audience and social media marketing allows targeting and retargeting. Publishing great content on social media profiles is the highlight of social media marketing and social media management tools help businesses to get the most out of social media marketing. Businesses publish content on social media platforms including Facebook and Twitter to generate traffic and drive sales. Social media of today is something more than just to broadcast content and social media analytics along with social media advertising is widely used today.

The core pillars of social media marketing are strategy, publishing, listening, analytics and advertising. Some businesses use social media marketing to build brand awareness while some of them use social media marketing for driving website traffic. Social media can also be used to generate engagement around a brand and create a community of likeminded individuals. According to social media marketing experts, Tumblr, Tik Tok, and Anchor are the upcoming social media channels. The list of leading social messaging platforms includes Facebook Messenger, Whatsapp, and We Chat.

Web Marketing Basics

Web marketing is essential to all businesses of today and web marketers unanimously agree that internet marketing is a very broad term. Any type of marketing activity executed online comes under the broad category of web marketing. Some of the most popular web marketing avenues include search engine marketing, Pay per Click, social media marketing, email marketing, content marketing, and online networking. Search engine optimization and paid search platforms like Google Ad Words are considered very crucial web marketing tactics. Extensive keyword research and writing great content are essential parts of Search Engine Optimization strategy.

Link building is a core component of SEO (Search Engine Optimization) and it helps a site to move up in search engine rankings. Yoast SEO is a free WordPress plug-in which can be used to optimize the site for search engine optimization. Pay per Click is a paid advertising strategy and PPC marketers are paid for clicks, conversions, actions taken, and impressions. Search ads allow internet marketers to show text ads to users who are actively searching for the keywords they have targeted. Google Adwords and Bing ads are the leading Pay per Click search advertisement platforms popular today. Facebook Ads, Instagram Ads, Google AdSense, and LinkedIn Ads are prominent display ads platforms.

Organic marketing and paid advertising are core components of social media marketing initiatives. Nurturing relationships with customers is the key objective of social media marketing and Facebook is unquestionably the most popular social media marketing platform. Twitter, Instagram, Pinterest, Tumblr and Periscope are other leading social media marketing channels. Email marketing is the process of nurturing leads through email communication with customers and it contains offers, product announcements and call to action. Mail Chimp is often referred as the best email marketing platform and content marketing involves the creation of blog posts, guest posts, ebooks, white papers and case studies.

Content marketing is often used in conjunction with search engine optimization and online networking is helpful in building relationships in online forums. Relationship building is the key objective of online networking and Facebook groups, LinkedIn groups, and Quora are some of the well known online communities. Online networking is a great way to get in front of potential clients and grow the business often for free. Well designed website acts as the foundation of web marketing and experts can be hired for designing high quality website. Hiring a professional web designer to create the website will cost around $1500 and hiring a copywriter will cost around $500.

Investing in PPC campaign may cost anywhere from $10 to $10000 and web marketing has become a necessity for businesses of today. Company website is the starting point for any form of web marketing and it is the business card of a company. Blog is often a good alternative for small businesses and not every company needs to create website with CMS. The quality of website content is the most important thing as far as web marketing is concerned. Content marketing has outnumbered traditional advertising such as television commercials and advertising banners.

Internet marketers should focus on well structured, high quality, interesting as well as informative content. Good content is the basis for success in web marketing and it is the foundation for Search Engine Optimization. An ideal website should feature content that is unique and fresh and web marketing takes time to implement. Good search engine rankings don't happen overnight and web marketing should follow a well defined strategy. The design aspect of a website is important in web marketing and it should be equipped with user friendliness. A company website should necessarily have an appealing design and clear navigation is an absolute must have for a website. The mobile optimization of company website is absolutely important and Google Analytics gives information about target group and online behaviour.

Website has become the most powerful marketing tool of today and it is the effective way to spread the word about a business. An ideal website for marketing purpose is equipped with clear call to action and up to date content. Smart SEO refers to understanding keywords, revising website structure, revising blog structure and creating content. Social media marketing should be used to its full potential in order to become a leader in web marketing. An ideal video campaign for business should include keyword rich headline, call to action and solid editorial message.

Solo entrepreneurs, small businesses and freelancers make use of web marketing strategies in the contemporary world. The basics of web marketing are easy to grasp and Search Engine Optimization helps businesses to attract customers in an organic way. An effective web marketing strategy includes different components like website design, search engine optimization, social media advertising, social media management, email marketing, Pay per Click and content marketing. The structure, colour, design, font style and content of a company website are very important to succeed in web marketing. According to top rated web marketing experts, an ideal company website should reflect brand style and personality. Website is a key extension of the business and it is an innovative idea to invest in a responsive website.

Right mix of design and functionality characterize a typical company website and website is an integral aspect of brand credibility. A typical company website needs to be fast and it should be secure with SSL (Secure Sockets Layer). A website needs to be mobile friendly and an easy to navigate website structure should be created. One of the simple ways to optimize website is by incorporating keywords in the site URL and another best SEO practice is to use keywords in title tags, Meta descriptions and heading tags.

Facebook Page is a great way to connect with customers and Facebook ads are more successful in gaining exposure for business. Instagram is the best social media channel to express business visually and it is growing extremely fast as a marketing channel. It has been estimated that 82% of B2B and B2C businesses use email marketing today and email marketing is one of the most effective web marketing channels. Pay per Click is immensely popular with advertisers because it helps them to attract quality traffic. The purpose of content marketing is to educate potential customers, establish authority and build loyalty. Web marketing is an ever growing field and a company needs experts well versed in SEO, SEM, PPC and SMO.

Web Marketing Best Practices

Incorporating more video content is a top rated web marketing best practice and it is to be noted that video consumption is growing very rapidly. Video marketing produces incredible results as a web marketing strategy and product videos have huge influence on the buyer persona. Creating amazing videos is a great way to reach more customers and engage them in an innovative way. Companies of today need to focus on giving customers a personalized experience and devising an effective content strategy is another web marketing best practice. Content marketing receives three times more leads than paid advertisings and effective content strategy is an inseparable element of web marketing.

Blogging is one of the best ways to implement effective content strategy and it is highly beneficial to B2B companies. Ace internet marketing experts reiterate that an excellent content strategy goes beyond blogging. Businesses of today need to focus on local SEO and 32% of consumers engage with brand video on YouTube, the game changer video sharing site. Having a video thumbnail in the search result can double the search traffic and web marketing will continue to evolve in the upcoming years too. Audience targeting, usage of fresh data, and Omni channel marketing are the web marketing best practices of 2019.

The content in a website should be easy to read, credible, accurate, compelling, interesting and authentic. Businesses will need to focus on SEO, SEM, local search marketing, content marketing, remarketing, responsive web design, social media marketing, email marketing, marketing automation, influencer marketing and video marketing. SEO continues to be the most important aspect of web marketing and hiring SEO expert is recommended. Recent news from the web marketing industry is that new HTTPS requirements impact SEO results. It is essential to update sites with HTTPS designation since Google labels HTTP sites as non secure.

Businesses need to hire a search engine marketing expert who has worked with Google ads and Search/display ads. The opportunity to customize multiple ad formats is a top rated feature of Facebook ads and listing the business in 'Google My Business' is a web marketing best practice. Online reviews play a key role in web marketing of the contemporary era and Yelp is a classic example. Inbound marketing techniques attract numerous customers and content marketing is helpful in attracting a targeted audience. The content featured in a website should be valuable, relevant, consistent, fresh as well as evergreen. Internet marketers should keep in the mind the famous adage 'content is king' and today's businesses need to focus on mobile content, native advertising and influencer marketing.

Entrepreneurs need to pay attention to mobile content since the usage of Smartphones increase on a day by day basis. Remarketing helps a business to stay more engaged, better promote brand with prospects and increase conversion. Making a website mobile responsive is one of the web marketing best practices in 2019 and beyond. Google favours responsive websites and email marketing continues to be a fantastic tool for generating leads. Email marketing is one of the most affordable methods of web marketing and the ability to add social share buttons and referral reward system is the illustrious feature of email marketing.

Following the web marketing best practices will help small and medium businesses to scale heights of excellence in business. Social media marketing is great for small businesses and big amount of money is not needed to carry out social media marketing campaign. Facebook marketing is a very lucrative opportunity for small and medium businesses of the contemporary age. 97% of B2B companies use Facebook and the top social media platforms used by B2B marketers include Facebook, Twitter, LinkedIn, YouTube, Instagram, and Pinterest. Internet marketers should have a crystal clear idea of how the combination of content marketing and web marketing works.

It is easier to reach specific target audience with the help of social media marketing and web marketing allows interacting with customers worldwide that traditional marketing can't offer. Businesses catering to millennial age range can choose Facebook marketing and companies that publish out of the box posts on Facebook can reap rich benefits. Instagram is an excellent web marketing tool and it can be used to interact with current and potential customers. The popularity of Instagram can be effectively used for promoting small businesses and hash tags are a key aspect of Instagram. Instagram has several additional features small businesses can take advantage of including Instagram stories and IGTV.

Consistency applies to all web marketing methods and Twitter is the ideal place for small and medium businesses. Twitter is a great place to promote blog posts and it can be used to stay ahead of the business competition. Pinterest is a huge marketing platform for small and medium businesses and it is a virtual bulletin board. The Pinterest is very visual and it is the best place to share eye catching graphics and aesthetic photographs. Both large and small companies utilize the services of LinkedIn and it is the social network for professionals.

LinkedIn is the leading social media channel for B2B marketers and content is one of the prime marketing strategies for LinkedIn. Email newsletters are effective and it is to be kept in mind that newsletter is different than a sales email. Blogging is one of the most important content marketing tactics and it can be used to engage audience along with attracting web traffic. Blog posts are a great way to get SEO keywords naturally into a website and regular blog posts keep a website fresh. A website should be updated with consistent blog posts since Google likes to see updated content.

The web marketing landscape encompassing SEO, Pay per Click, social media marketing and content marketing is witnessing a dramatic shift. The web marketing success is all about creating compelling content combined with marketing automation tools. Personalized content such as videos and Infographics will become key components of web marketing strategy of upcoming years. Colourful, attention grabbing and insightful content is a core feature of any content marketing campaign of today. It has been found that there is a link between regularly updated content and increased customer interaction. The content in a website should be customer centric and personalized content marketing has become need of the hour.

Facebook Marketing

Facebook marketing is defined as creating a Facebook page as a communication channel to attract customers. Facebook is used as a marketing tool by brands, local businesses, famous personalities, and non profit organizations. Any brand including food, electronics, restaurants, and home goods can be promoted by the social media tycoon Facebook. Celebrities, authors, artists, musicians, and columnists make use of Facebook for brand promotion. Charities, public service campaigns, and social welfare clubs can leverage the capabilities of Facebook.

Facebook page is often linked to a company web page and consistency of communication is important as far as Facebook marketing is concerned. Businesses should regularly post new content on Facebook in order to attract more customers and every business needs a Facebook presence in the contemporary era. Facebook is the largest social network in the universe in the contemporary age and it is the internet for many of us. Facebook marketing involves understanding of the goals of customers and it helps businesses to distribute quality content. According to renowned web marketing experts, Facebook marketing requires a consistent as well as long term commitment.

How to Setup Facebook Page?

Create Facebook page

Add photos

Include product description

Create username for page

Add page Call to Action

Organize page tabs

Verify page

Around 70 billion businesses in the universe market through Facebook page and the Facebook page is equivalent to business profile. The profile picture will serve as a primary visual for Facebook page and Facebook is a venue for businesses to market themselves through interaction with customers. Facebook is a very powerful marketing tool for small businesses and it is a very helpful tool for building brand identity. Facebook page is a great free marketing tool for businesses and it lets businesses identify themselves. A typical Facebook page gives a better sense of the personality and character of an online/offline business. Images, links and videos can be shared in the Facebook page of a typical business organization or brand.

Facebook ads are referred as marketplace advertisements and they include headline with copy, image, click through link to Facebook page, and Facebook app. The list of key features in Facebook advertising include demographic targeting, ad testing and built in ad performance measurement tools. It has been estimated that Facebook ads have a click through rate of 0.051% and it has an average CPC of $0.80. The cost of a Facebook advertising campaign can depend on numerous factors including competitions and targeting options. Running Facebook contests, sweepstakes, and promotions is another Facebook advertising tactic.

Sponsored stories are a prominent type of Facebook ads that showcase a user's interaction such as Facebook like. Facebook Exchange lets tech savvy advertisers take advantage of ad retargeting on Facebook. Increasing brand awareness, increasing community engagement, lead generation and increase in web traffic are the primary goals of Facebook marketers. A business can reach target audience more efficiently by well planned Facebook marketing strategy. Facebook is an excellent source to improve business reach and the Facebook can better nurture customers. The effective usage of Facebook marketing paves the way towards more efficient recruiting and sharing valuable content that connects with fans is the major feature of Facebook marketing.

How to Create a Facebook Marketing Campaign?
Define the target audience

Set goals

Consider the content mix

Create Facebook business page

Start posting

Ramp up Facebook likes and followers

Create Facebook group

Incorporate Facebook ads

Track the marketing campaign

Facebook marketers need to get familiar with Facebook demographics and Facebook Audience Insight can be used to get details about potential customers. The goals of Facebook marketing will differ for every business and Facebook marketing goals are measurable. Using Facebook for business is all about building relationships and the ideal Facebook marketing strategy will be sales focused. The algorithm of Facebook will penalize brands that push sales hard and it is important to post consistently in Facebook.

It is an innovative idea to create content calendar for Facebook marketing and businesses working with a limited budget are the key beneficiaries of Facebook marketing. Businesses don't need billions of followers to start a Facebook page and choosing a search friendly page name is a Facebook marketing best practice. Facebook marketers say that the cover and profile photo of a Facebook page should look absolutely stunning. Facebook text post is the most basic type of Facebook post and it can be used to spark engagement on a Facebook page. Adding photos to Facebook posts will significantly boost the number of Facebook likes as well as shares. Including graphics, illustration, GIF or any other visual in a Facebook post is a great and novel idea.

Facebook video post is often compelling and videos start to play automatically in the Facebook news feed. Longer videos have more chances of becoming a bumper hit among internet users and Buzzfeed's tasty recipe videos are an excellent example. Video post is an important way to connect with customers today and Facebook live video is a great way to interact with followers. Facebook live video is the perfect format to share announcements in real time and linked content post has become quite familiar in Facebook.

The content posted to Facebook should be highly shareable and it is the best way to expand organic reach. Facebook marketers should essentially focus on providing content that enhances customer relationships with one another. Facebook group should be added to every Facebook marketing campaign and it is the meeting place of likeminded individuals of the internet era. The Facebook ad is for specific and targeted audience and businesses looking to have a presence on social media should embrace Facebook marketing. Facebook page is a place where people can find businesses online, learn about business and connect with businesses.

Creating a Facebook page is very straightforward and building a Facebook page for business is super easy. 41% of USA based small businesses use Facebook as a part of their marketing campaign and Facebook marketing has become one of the biggest digital channels. Facebook offers numerous paid and organic tools for business promotion as well as branding. It is important to look beyond click or impression in order to see how successful a Facebook campaign is. Facebook ads are a great way to engage with audience on the social media channel and it encourages people to enter into the sales funnel.

Web Marketing Platform for Small Businesses

Some of the best web marketing platforms for small businesses include Hub Spot Marketing, Rank Active, Exponea, Moz, Active Campaign, iContact Pro, and Wishpond. Hub Spot is an award winning software and it has transformed the way businesses attract, engage and delight customers. The Hub Spot helps companies to create a web presence and convert online traffic into leads that can be tracked. Hub Spot Marketing Hub is designed to serve B2B and B2B customers in the verticals of software, technology, retail and construction. It offers diverse tools to attract more visitors, convert more leads, close deals and delight customers.

Integrated blogging, content creation tools, and built in Search Engine optimization are the splendid features of Hub Spot. Hub Spot is the best example of world class marketing automation and it comprises Marketing Hub, Sales Hub, Service Hub, and free CRM. The Hub Spot features every marketing tool in one place and it depicts the pinnacle of excellence in business software. It is an undisputable fact that Hub Spot is the best software for automating customer database and sales process. The mailing list of Hub Spot is a top rated one and Hub Spot is the best marketing software for small businesses and educational institutions.

Rank Active is software built for Search Engine Optimization agencies, internet marketers and business owners. Competitor analysis, keyword research tools, auditing, Google Analytics integration, keyword tracking, localization and rank tracking are the key SEO features of Rank Active. Rank Active is a multifarious internet marketing tool and ease of use and excellent customer service are the glorious features of Rank Active. The Rank Active is a comprehensive SEO tool and awesome rank tracking plans punctuate the Rank Active software. Ease of reporting and the speed of software make Rank Active a popular option among web marketers.

Rank Active is an All-in-One SEO platform and the professional and optimal versions of Rank Active are priced at $70 and $150 respectively per month. The Rank Active offers the best value for money and it accommodates the growing needs of SEO. Its keyword research tool is very useful and it is the best SEO software suite at an affordable price range. Rank Active is generally attractive web marketing software and it is a solid web marketing tool for small businesses. It is equipped with strong features like back links explore, rank tracker, website analytics, and site auditor. The Rank Active sends weekly report to the inbox and the inclusive SEO software auto generates keywords.

The ultimate goal of Customer Relationship Management software is the management of sales pipeline. The selection of ideal web marketing software is dependent upon numerous factors like ongoing cost, features, usability, upfront cost and integrations. The field of web marketing software is ever expanding and a marketing automation tool enables marketers to make an informed business decision. Progressive profiling, targeted email campaigns, integration of website, CRM and marketing automation are the rich features of ideal web marketing software. All in one inbound marketing software are always in high demand and it can be used to launch an effective marketing campaign.

The list of top 5 free marketing automation software include Mail Chimp, Mautic, SendinBlue, Send Pulse and Zoho campaigns. The free version of Mail Chimp is decorated with extensive email and social media marketing capabilities. Mail Chimp free version offers A/B testing module, segmentation, email automation, social media management and landing page designer. Setting up Mail Chimp is very easy and detailed reporting functionality is a unique feature of Mail Chimp. The free version of Mail Chimp supports up to 2000 subscribers and businesses need to upgrade if they want to manage more subscribers. The Mail Chimp is recommended for small and midsized businesses and it features Android as well as iOS versions too.

Mautic is a top rated open source marketing automation solution for small and medium sized businesses. Various marketing features like email marketing module, account based marketing, website tracking, social media management and landing page designer are incorporated in Mautic. The biggest benefit of Mautic is the diversity of features it offers and it provides content marketing tools too. According to prominent software reviewers, Mautic's email templates are very easy to use as well as customize. It is available free of cost since it is an open source solution and there are no mobile apps available for Mautic.

Email marketing, content marketing, SMS and social media marketing are the prime features of Mautic. Some level of technical knowledge is required to setup, configure and customize the Mautic software. SendinBlue is a cloud based marketing automation software with glowing reputation and impeccable credentials. Workflow editor, personalized email campaigns, web page tracking, and built in library of email templates are the elegant specialties of SendinBlue. Reviewers said that SendinBlue is perfect for newsletter campaigns as it offers lots of templates and drag and drop functionality. Simple email campaign interface is the most talked about feature of SendinBlue, the torch bearer of innovation in marketing automation.

SendPulse is the multichannel solution for emails, newsletters, push notifications as well as SMS marketing. The free version of SendPulse consists of email automation, email templates and A/B testing module. Its low cost of upgrade makes it popular among small and medium sized businesses of today. The SendPulse offers numerous upgrade options for SMS marketing and web push notification. Small and medium businesses prefer SendPulse because it offers email marketing, transactional emails, SMS marketing and browser push notification campaigns.

According to the information available from the market, Zoho campaign is a cloud based email marketing solution designed for small businesses. Zoho has gained resplendent victory as web marketing software and its free version includes customizable email templates, segmentation tools, social media marketing and customized reporting. Numerous report templates offered in the free version of Zoho makes it popular among web marketing managers. The free version of Zoho campaigns lets users connect with G Suite, Survey Monkey, Shopify and Eventbrite. Free version of Zoho campaign allows sending up to 12000 emails per month and it features Android and iOS versions. Sales teams depending heavily on email marketing and email campaigns can reap the benefits of Zoho Campaigns. Choosing the right email marketing software will have a big impact on the success of email marketing campaign.

Web Marketing Software

There are many requirements for the selection of typical web marketing software and social media marketing and marketing automation are the desirable traits of web marketing software. Hootsuite, Sprinklr and Buffer are leading social media management software and distribution channel available today. Social media is a distribution channel for content marketing and ideal web marketing software is used for growing revenue and streamlining operations. The list of top web marketing software include Ahrefs, Aiva, Basecamp, Beacon, Browser Stack, Buzz Stream, Calendly, Ceros, Click Up, Drift and Google Analytics.

The selection of web marketing software will ultimately depend on the type of business and the kind of customers targeting. Email marketing is one of the most effective web marketing methods and it can give Return on Investment up to 4300%. The SEO keyword tool of Ahrefs is one of the best search engine optimization tools and it is the most recommended SEO tool. It can be used to find the most linked content within the niche and it is the favourite tool of web marketers when it comes to keyword research, rank tracking, SEO audit and competitor research. Ahrefs is instrumental in getting a site ranked for different keywords and Google Search Console is a top SEO tool.

Google Search Console is offered free for everyone with a website and it can be used to monitor website presence in Google Search Engine Results Pages. The SEO checker tool of Google Search Console can be used to optimize for better performance in Google search engine results page. SEM Rush has become a favourite among the web marketing community and domain vs domain analysis is the top rated feature of SEM Rush. It is equipped with an on page SEO checker tool and SEM rush is one of the best search engine optimization tools. The SEO keyword tool of KW Finder can be used to find long tail keywords having a low level of competition.

SEO experts utilize the KW Finder to find the best keywords and run analysis reports on back links. Moz is a SEO software which can be used to get raving customer reviews and it is always up to date with the search algorithms of Google. The Moz is a full service web marketing powerhouse and its page optimization feature is the favourite of internet marketers. Uber Suggest is an excellent keyword tracking tool and it can be used to find the keywords and search intent behind them. The list of metrics included in Uber Suggest keyword tool include keyword volume, competition, Cost per Click, and seasonal trends.

Some of the most popular web marketing software includes Yoast, Google Adwords, Google Analytics, Canva Business and MeetEdgar. The tools of Hub Spot are helpful in growing business and it can be used to setup web forms, pop up forms and live chat software. Advanced marketing automation capabilities is another well known feature of Hub Spot marketing software. Ahrefs impresses web marketers with its exquisite features and it is a fantastic tool for competitive analysis. The Ahrefs is robust web marketing software and the Yoast is a free WordPress plug-in which is used to optimize content for search engines.

The most widely used web marketing solutions include CRM, video conferencing solution, email service, marketing automation platform, data visualization solutions and Content Management System. The most popular email marketing tools include Mail Chimp, Constant Contact, Campaigner, Campaign Monitor, and Get Response. Some of the renowned marketing automation software includes Auto Pilot, Marketo, Pardot and Eloqua. Popular web analytics solutions include Crazy Egg, Eye Quant, Google Analytics, Hot Jar and Kissmetrics Analytics. The list of top rated content management software includes WordPress, Joomla, Drupal, Wix and Squarespace. Instapage, VWO and Optimizely are best examples of website optimization software solutions. Uber Suggest, Google Keyword Planner, and Yoast are the best web marketing tools for SEO and blogging.

Top web marketing software for analytics and data include Google Analytics, Sumo Me, and platform based social media analytics. Best web marketing software for visual design includes the elegant Canva, Animoto and Freepik. Google Analytics is a must for every web marketing company to scale business and it features all the important information about the website like audience demographics, popular keywords and actions taken. Platform based social media analytics are the free analytics tools built into the social media platforms of Facebook, Twitter and YouTube. Google Keyword Planner is a frequently used blog content tool and Yoast increases the chances of getting ranked well in search engines.

Promo Republic is an inclusive social media tool that helps businesses to run social media marketing on auto pilot. Scheduling, content creation, social monitoring and collaboration are the key features of Promo Republic. MeetEdgar is one of the best web marketing software for evergreen content and Hootsuite features an easy way to schedule posts. Tail wind is one of the best available options for managing Pinterest account and it can be used to build huge following on Pinterest. Social Pilot is a full fledged social media marketing tool for professionals, small teams and agencies.

The well known features of Social Pilot include bulk scheduling capability, content calendar, content curation, and RSS feed automation. Active Campaign is the best platform for email marketing, marketing automation and sales CRM software. Automation of lead generation and client communication are the key objectives of Hatchbuck and its CRM is designed for small businesses. Omnisend is a feature rich omnichannel marketing automation tool for ecommerce and it allows businesses reach customers based on their action. Canva is an essential visual design tool for web marketing and beautiful photos can be created using Canva.

Amazing varieties of pictorial colours, logos and fonts are the unique selling proposition of Canva. Animoto is used for the creation of professional slideshow videos with music, text, and visual effects. Freepik gives access to more than one million photos and icons for monthly subscription fee. Design Wizard is a top rated graphic design tool for web marketing and high quality images can be personalized using Design Wizard. The Design Wizard is used by internet marketers, SEO companies, business owners, social media marketers and solo entrepreneurs. Custom colour palette, free font library, and resize feature are the spectacular features of Design Wizard. Another noted feature of Design Wizard is that it can be easily integrated with Hubspot, Marketo, Intercom and Buffer.

Youtube Marketing

YouTube has become an essential tool for internet marketers and it has more than a billion active users. The YouTube is an extensive web marketing platform and YouTube can improve SEO and overall web presence. YouTube allows internet marketers to showcase unique content and YouTube marketing is an excellent tool for brands. It is a very well known fact that maintaining a YouTube channel takes lots of time and planning. YouTube hosts only video content and creating engaging and shareable content on YouTube is important.

The YouTube channel is an extension of business brand and the channel name should be consistent with overall branding. YouTube channel trailer should be kept very short and optimizing the metadata of YouTube video is the first SEO step. According to successful YouTube marketers, the title and description of video should be optimized. Video transcript can improve SEO and #hash tags should be included in video title and descriptions. YouTube video thumbnail has a large impact on the amount of clicks and 90% of the top performing YouTube videos have custom thumbnails. Customer testimonial videos, product demonstration videos, explainer videos, thought leader interviews, project reviews, YouTube live, video blogs and event videos are the most popular types of videos on YouTube.

High ranking in search results and having a large subscriber base are the ideal features of YouTube videos. Sharing YouTube videos on social media channels is an excellent idea and YouTube provides a shortened video for posting. YouTube videos can be marketed on company/personal websites as well as blogs along with adding a YouTube follow icon to the website. The YouTube videos can be embedded in blog posts or website and they can be shared with relevant email lists. Sending an email newsletter with video content is another great way to keep contacts engaged and high level marketing strategy is required for YouTube videos.

YouTube channel branding should be kept consistent with all other social media accounts and real people can be featured in YouTube videos. Its video thumbnail should accurately represent video content and call to action should be included in every YouTube video. YouTube marketers can create playlists featuring different videos and YouTube videos should be produced on a regular basis. Creating interesting content, optimizing the content for SEO, and sharing it across different platforms are three vital YouTube marketing tactics. Understanding YouTube Analytics is very straightforward and YouTube marketers should focus on targeting one goal per video.

The ultimate objective of a typical YouTube video is to increase brand awareness and YouTube is unquestionably a great platform for building brand awareness. YouTube marketing is an excellent way to build credibility and YouTube analytics shows how users found the content. The YouTube analytics showcases top line performance metrics, engagement metrics, demographics, traffic sources and popular content. Watch time is a YouTube ranking factor and video with higher watch time will get higher rankings. There are several paid options for promoting video on YouTube and YouTube uses a cost per view model.

Video discovery ads and in-stream ads are two types of YouTube ads and video discovery ads appear on YouTube home page. YouTube is the best platform for showcasing video content in an interesting and engaging way. YouTube marketers should keep in mind that the YouTube viewers want to get engaged and entertained. The YouTube is an incredibly powerful marketing tool since it is one of the biggest websites in the whole world. YouTube provides huge potential for business outreach and publishing quality content consistently on YouTube is quite important. Good YouTube marketing plan is an absolute essentiality for every web marketer and YouTube marketing is highly popular because video marketing is the current trend.

YouTube video is one of the best performing forms of content and they can be repurposed for email marketing campaigns and landing pages. It is a great platform for B2B companies and lead generation is the number one business objective of YouTube videos. The objectives of YouTube marketing should be specific, measurable, attainable, time bound and relevant. Consistency is very important in YouTube just like blogging and successful YouTubers stick to a strict publishing schedule. It seems that listicles, how to videos, behind the scene videos, product videos, case studies and interviews are the most popular types of content on YouTube.

Engagement is the most important part of YouTube marketing and YouTube marketing is an attractive promotional tool since it is one of the biggest search engines in the universe. There are numerous factors that influence the ranking of YouTube videos and some of them are under the control of YouTubers. Channels, video headlines, video descriptions, video transcript, watch time, thumbnail image, and subscriber numbers are some of the YouTube ranking factors. Using the right tags in YouTube video is very important and YouTube also looks at the engagement of channels. Tube Buddy is a renowned YouTube SEO tool and it features YouTube keyword research tools, tag explorer, and keyword rank tracking.

Optimizing the video content is an important part of YouTube marketing strategy and keyword research is a great tool for finding new video ideas.

Core Pillars of YouTube Marketing Strategy

Strategize YouTube presence ahead of time

Create different types of videos

Take the time to engage with customers and subscribers

Optimize channels and videos for YouTube search engine

YouTube marketing is the secret to content marketing in 2019 and it is essential for businesses of all sizes.

It is absolutely important to create compelling titles for YouTube videos and keywords in the title tell Google crawlers what the video is about. The length of YouTube video titles should not exceed 60 characters and readers should see the whole title in a glance. According to victorious YouTube bloggers, it is important to create clear and descriptive title for videos. Effective thumbnails make YouTube viewers click right away and it makes the YouTube channel more recognizable. Short descriptions and relevant images should be included in the thumbnail of a typical YouTube video.

Ideas to come up with a good video title

Identify a central idea of video

Search for short as well as descriptive keyword phrases

Choose titles which answer important questions

Future of Web Marketing

The future of web marketing is definitely bright and traditional marketing will get completely taken over by web marketing in the next decade. Web marketing will continue to be a great career path in the upcoming years and there will be plenty of job opportunities in the web marketing arena in the future. Paid media, SEO, content marketing, and social media will witness dramatic advancements in the next ten years. Artificial intelligence will have a big impact in the web marketing industry of tomorrow and video content will become a huge hit in the next decade. Personalization will become the key aspect of content marketing in 2019 and big data will influence web marketing of upcoming years.

It is expected that video content will become the most popular form of content by the year 2020 and beyond. Video will be used as a digital marketing tool in the coming years and personalized video messaging has become quite popular. 360 degree video content will become a key part of marketing campaigns of 2020 and virtual reality will influence the digital marketing arena. Influencer marketing systems will get automated soon and it will become more popular than word of mouth marketing. The growing population of tech savvy internet users will revitalize the web marketing segment and it has been reported that artificial intelligence will power customer segmentation and retargeting in the future.

Artificial intelligence offers infinite possibilities in the web marketing field and marketers will use artificial intelligence for product recommendations and campaign optimization. AI (Artificial Intelligence) will be used for audience expansion, audience targeting, product recommendations and campaign optimization. Artificial Intelligence will be a key tool in improving customer service and it increases customer lifetime value too. The Internet of Things will have a big impact in the web marketing industry of upcoming years. Geo targeting and infinite possibilities for personalization are the hallmarks of web marketing strategy of 2020.

Blockchain is a groundbreaking trend in the digital marketing field and mobile devices, personalization technologies, Internet of Things, predictive analytics, big data, artificial intelligence, augmented reality, virtual reality, wearable technology, and smart visual assistants will have the biggest impact on web marketing of tomorrow. Combining Artificial Intelligence with content personalization offers incredible opportunities for internet marketers. According to chief marketing officers of renowned companies, the top web marketing channels of 2020 include social media, web, mobile apps, mobile web, email, direct mail, television, print and radio. Digital technologies are helpful in measuring key metrics for web marketing and optimizing for mobile will be a key web marketing trend in 2020. Improving UX experience and content diversification will be the key elements of web marketing strategy in the next year.

Video marketing is the next big thing in web marketing and YouTube has become bigger than Facebook. More internet marketers are producing videos for social media vehicles of Instagram, Facebook and LinkedIn. According to a research report by the industry major Cisco, 81% of all the traffic will be video by 2021. Blog posts, images and podcasts will become the key elements of content marketing strategy in the imminent years. Automation will bring a new era of modernization in the web marketing landscape and chat bot is an emerging trend in web marketing field.

Optimizing the website for mobile will become an absolute must have in the coming years and 2020 will witness many machine learning victories in the web marketing field. Content marketing will get diversified soon including articles, blog posts, video, podcasting, and Infographics. Web marketing companies need to hire more video producers and graphic designers as a part of their marketing strategy. Creating a well organized website and conceptualizing high quality content are integral parts of web marketing strategy of today and tomorrow. Web marketing tools like Moz, Ahrefs, Majestic and SEM Rush will continue to evolve in the future too. It has been pointed out that smaller brands will make a huge impact by social media marketing in 2020.

The web marketing field is constantly changing and the web marketing strategy of future will concentrate on customer experience, functionality and targeted advertising. The innovations in web marketing are refined through the use of artificial intelligence and the field of artificial intelligence in the context of web marketing is very broad. Ecommerce major Amazon is equipped with built in Artificial Intelligence features that help with product recommendations. AI will get used in content creation, voice recognition, face recognition, chat bots, digital assistants and targeted marketing strategies. Artificial intelligence implementation in web marketing paves the way towards interactive and personalized purchasing experience.

Artificial Intelligence powered personal assistants will become integral parts of web marketing in 2020. The usage of social media in web marketing will see a huge shift in the next decade and Blockchain has become a hot topic of discussion in digital marketing. Chat bots improve the UX for digital marketers and they will soon evolve into a versatile digital marketing tool. Influencer marketing will continue to evolve in the B2B and B2C sectors and the web marketing arena will get revitalized in the next decade. AI driven content marketing strategy will become a reality in the next few years and it has huge potential in web marketing.

It is expected that chat bots will become a customer service standard and it will soon replace live agents. Web marketing will become more personalized and conversational in the upcoming days of massive internet explosion. Artificial Intelligence is used in digital advertising too and Google is already running ads empowered by Artificial intelligence. Augmented reality will become a web marketing opportunity in the next decade and it can be used to reach more customers. Video marketing will be a powerful medium of marketing in the upcoming years too and the combination of video and augmented reality offers great opportunities in the web marketing field.

It is crucial to stay ahead of the trends in web marketing and implement innovative web marketing strategies. Customer experience, micro moments, functionality, and targeted advertising are the latest trends in web marketing. The implementation of Artificial Intelligence in web marketing will lead to interactive and personalized buying experience. According to prominent internet marketing experts, a combination of virtual reality, augmented reality and mixed reality will bring new era of change in the web marketing industry. Brand focused chat bots is the latest trend in web marketing and web marketers should consider speech recognition and voice search for brand building.

Search Engine Marketing

Search engine marketing is an effective web marketing strategy which can be used to grow business in a competitive marketplace. It is one of the best ways to promote products and search engine marketing is the practice of marketing business using paid advertisements. Search engine marketing ads are known as Pay per Click ads and text based ads and product listing ads are two types of Pay per Click ads. The search engine marketing is a very powerful way to grow business and it refers to paid search marketing. Search engine optimization and search engine marketing are key components of web marketing strategy.

The search engine optimization is the best way to drive traffic at the top of the funnel and search engine marketing is a cost effective way to drive conversions at the bottom of the funnel. Keywords act as the foundation of search engine marketing and search engine marketing is also referred as paid search. Search engine marketing has become a crucial part of web marketing strategy and advertisers pay for impressions in search engine marketing. Results are immediate with search engine marketing and it is considered as the fastest way to attract traffic to a website.

Steps Involved in Search Engine Marketing

Conduct keyword research and select a list of keywords

Select a geographic location for the ad to be displayed

Create a text based ad

Bid on a price

Text only advertisements are very easy to produce and Google Ads and Bing Ads are the two most popular types of search ad networks. The Google Ads consists of two networks: Google Search Network and Google Display Network. The Google search network comprises search related websites owned by Google and the Google Display Network contains properties such as YouTube, Blogger and Gmail. The most common terms used in search engine marketing are paid search ads, paid search advertising, Pay per Click, cost per click and cost per thousand impressions. Google Ads is the most popular paid search platform and it is important to understand paid and unpaid means of search engine marketing to understand what search engine marketing is.

SEM (Search Engine Marketing) can be used to draw in more customers, improve SERP rankings, and boost search engine presence. Search Engine Marketing is one of the best ways to reach more customers and it has become a necessity to invest in SEM. The list of best SEM tools includes SEM Rush, Google Trends, Keyword.io, Google Ads Keyword Planner, and Spy Fu. The key functionalities provided by SEM Rush are keyword research, keyword rank tracking, site auditing, and traffic analysis. SEM Rush is a great tool for finding long tail keywords organically and it can be used for various web marketing initiatives.

Google Trends allow web marketers to track search volume for particular keyword across specific language or time. It is a fantastic tool for Search Engine Marketing efforts and the ability to tap into Amazon, Fiverr, Bing, YouTube, Google, Instagram and Twitter is the great feature of keyword.io. The free version of keyword.io can be used to generate 750 long tail keywords and keyword suggestions for a single search term. The Google Keyword Planner can be used to research relevant keywords for business and web marketers can monitor SEO rankings on Google, Bing and Yahoo using SpyFu. Both search engine optimization and search engine marketing terms are often used interchangeably.

SEM is a web marketing method that increases the visibility of a site through organic search results and advertising. Search engine marketing includes search engine optimization and other web marketing methods. Search engine optimization is an essential component of search engine marketing and ace internet marketers opine that organic SEO is the best approach. True search engine marketing cannot succeed without the usage of organic search engine optimization. There are many situations where Pay per Click makes more sense than search engine optimization. Pay per Click campaign takes less time than search engine optimization and organic SEO takes long time to show results.

Search engine marketing (SEM) and search engine optimization (SEO) exist as two separate entities today. A business can reap rich benefits if they employ both search engine optimization and search engine marketing. The Search Engine Marketing is particularly helpful in brand building and growing the client base. The most well known search engine marketing platforms are Google Ads, Bing Ads and Yahoo Search Ads. Although all SEM platforms utilize a Pay per Click model, not all Pay per Click are search engine marketing.

The answer to the question, 'do keywords still matter for SEM?' is a very big 'Yes' and keywords are important in SEM just like SEO. In-depth keyword research is a vital component of running a successful search engine marketing campaign. According to top rated web marketers, choosing the right keywords can make or break a typical search engine marketing campaign. All prominent search engine marketing platforms work on a bidding system and advertisers bid on certain keywords and audiences. Majority of the Search Engine Marketing Platforms take the quality of advertisements into account. Investing in search engine marketing will be a wise business decision and successful business organizations integrate SEM into marketing mix. Traditional SEM is made up of two components: organic search engine optimization and Pay per Click advertising.

Google Ads placement targeting, social media marketing and integrated vertical search impact search engine marketing. Pay per Click has the ability to advertise across the entire internet and it is not just limited to search engines. The most popular integrated vertical search is Google's universal search and major search engines have adopted similar search formats. Most of the search advertising platforms of today are results driven and all search engine marketing methods are measurable. Testing, measuring and tweaking are three prime components of search engine marketing initiatives.

It is a well known fact that search engine marketing is a very fast and growing branch of web marketing. Search engine marketing is one of the targeted methods of getting the right visitors to a website. SEM is a very effective way for small and medium businesses to reach customers and increase revenues. Search Engine Marketing leverages the power of search engines like Google to reach potential customers. The Search Engine Marketing is also called as paid search ads, paid advertising and Pay per Click. Social media marketing and search engine marketing can work together to create brand awareness. SEM is often perceived as a primary marketing method and nothing can drive more leads and sales than SEM.

Making Money Online

Some of the top ways to make money online are blogging, affiliate marketing, becoming a YouTuber, and website flipping. Blogging is a lucrative way to make money online and creating a blog is super easy with the WordPress. Quality content is the most important thing as far as blogging is concerned and visual elements and images are core components of the blogs of contemporary age. Some popular categories of blogs include personal finance, online business, fitness, investing, real estate, careers and freelancing. B2B blogs have become very popular today and WordPress is the best content management system recommended for blogging.

One of the most popular ways to make money with blogging is by placing ads on the website and CPC ads and CPM ads are two types of ads in blogging. Google AdSense is the most popular ad network for making money with blogging and bloggers can make money by selling private ads, selling digital products and using the blogging as content marketing tool for business. According to well known bloggers, the best blogging platforms for making money are WordPress and Wix. WordPress is unquestionably the best blogging software and CMS (Content Management System). Domain name, web hosting and setting up WordPress account are the things needed to setup a WordPress blog.

It is to be kept in mind that blogging is not a get rich quick scheme and making a social media marketing strategy for blogs is recommended. Marketing plays a crucial role in blog promotion and blogging brings abundance of benefits to the business. A blogging marketing plan should include publishing schedule, target audience, content auditing, social media strategy, paid content advertising, keyword research, costing and marketing goals. Some of the best tips to boost blog traffic include building a Twitter following, linking the blog to Facebook, creating an email list, hosting a webinar and publishing great content. Non tech savvy users can create a blog with WordPress and the self hosted WordPress is the best option for making money with blogging.

The self hosted WordPress can be easily customized and a web domain typically costs $15 per year. Bluehost is a leader in WordPress hosting and customizing the look and feel of the blog is an exciting advantage of WordPress. Themes control the visual appearance of WordPress and there are numerous paid and free WordPress themes. Simplicity in design characterizes a typical WordPress theme and WordPress plug-ins are apps that allow adding new features to a website. According to skilled web developers, a WordPress blog enhances customer experience and boosts conversions.

Affiliate marketing is one of the easiest ways of making money online and different affiliate marketing platforms use different payment terms like Pay per Click, Pay per Sale, and Pay per Lead. The affiliate marketing is a passive income source and promoting profitable products is the key to success in affiliate marketing. Visitors can be attracted to an affiliate website by paid advertising, free advertising, article marketing and email marketing. Mobile affiliate marketing is gaining prominence as an affiliate marketing method and affiliate marketing is really attractive since it offers a constant stream of passive income. The most popular affiliate marketplaces include Share a Sale, Click Bank, CJ Affiliate, Impact and Flex Offers.

Popular online retailers like Amazon, EBay, Etsy, Walmart, and Ali Express have affiliate programs. Amazon Associates is a renowned affiliate program of the ecommerce giant and site wide commissions and high conversions are the key features of Amazon Associates program. Affiliate marketing is considered as one of the best ways to make money online since it does not include any product creation. Affiliate marketers will get access to commission and sales statistics of an affiliate program. Affiliate marketing is one of the fastest growing and best ways of making money online in the internet age.

Being a YouTuber has become a glowing, rewarding, exciting, creative and successful career today. Combination of perseverance, patience, and enthusiasm are needed to become a successful YouTuber. Some of the well known YouTubers are experts in creating beauty, fashion and travel video content. YouTubers should add a personal touch to their video content and they should focus on content diversification. Renowned YouTubers never make compromise on the quality of video/audio and a good camera is the basic investment for YouTube video blogging.

High quality DSLR or Smartphone camera is essential to become a rock star YouTube blogger of today. The success of YouTubers reaffirm that 'light, camera, action' is not limited to film studios in Hollywood. Successful YouTubers will have a basic knowledge of photography, filming, editing, and film making. They take short term courses in photography, videography, filming, editing as well as film making. YouTubers need to keep up with the changes in YouTube as the video sharing platform is evolving constantly. YouTube video bloggers should understand that a YouTube video reflects their personality and creativity. Renowned YouTubers are master experts in the personalization of video blogs and YouTube offers lucrative career opportunities. YouTube channel acts like the mirror of a YouTuber and an ideal YouTube video should be visually attractive.

YouTube video blogging is the new age blogging and it has become a very lucrative career among the youth. An established social media presence is helpful in the career as a YouTube video blogger and YouTube video blogging is a career with unlimited earning potential. Becoming a YouTuber is a most sought after career today and the major share of a YouTube vlogger comes from lucrative brand partnership deals. It is important to select the niche wisely before starting a YouTube channel and the best way to become a YouTube blogger is by choosing a niche the vlogger is passionate about. A YouTuber should have a clear idea about his target audience and coming up with quality content is the number one YouTube vlogging tip.

According to well known YouTubers, consistency is the most important thing as far as YouTube video blogging is concerned. The YouTube vlogging camera and microphone should be of top quality and a good YouTube vlog is about the authenticity of vlogger. Video editing is the key part of YouTube vlogging and there are lots of free video editing tools available. Right keywords should be used in order to get more exposure for the video and using the right keyword guarantees higher ranking in YouTube search results. One of the key tips to increase the click through rates of YouTube video is to use intriguing video titles.

Article Marketing

Article marketing is a marketing strategy used by web marketers to acquire new visitors and increase sales. The article marketing involves writers and publishers as primary participants and it is a subset of content marketing. The basic purpose of article marketing is to attract online audience and article marketing is very helpful in the SEO efforts. Article marketers are often independent writers, online publishers, bloggers, thought leaders, and columnists. Product manufacturers, service providers, and franchise companies make use of article marketing.

Examples of businesses that use article marketing include health and wellness providers, scientific journals, online retailers, resellers, travel companies and hotels. According to web marketing luminaries, article marketing is one of the cheapest and fastest ways to promote content online. Keyword search optimization is an inseparable element of article marketing and article marketing should address the needs of niche target audience. Some of the most popular article directories are Ezine Articles, Helium, Articles Base, Go Articles and Article Dash Board. It has been pointed out that well known content aggregators include Digg, Reddit, Slash Dot and Stumble Upon. The best feature of article marketing is that it is highly customizable and companies can effectively reach target markets using article marketing. An article marketing campaign is based on content relevancy and properly executed article marketing campaign can attract millions of new visitors.

The first step in article marketing is to identify specific target niches and create a list of topics that would engage readers. Writers use by-line, link to content and few description lines in their article marketing campaigns. Social media manager, marketing manager, content writer, copywriter, and social media strategist are the professionals involved in article marketing initiatives. Article marketing is very essential for building a network of incoming links that drive website traffic. Articles can get top ten placements in leading search engines including Google, Yahoo and Bing.

The articles can be distributed in number of ways including self publishing on website, submitting to sites dedicated to specific topic, emailing quality articles to high traffic websites and submitting to popular article directories. Online article marketing can improve organic search results in a number of ways and it improves visibility for target keyword phrases. Article marketing assists in building brand awareness and it makes a website more unique as well as useful. Effective article marketing is a key business strategy for majority of the enterprises and it is not just submitting articles to article directories. Article marketing is about publishing high quality articles in leading article directories and increased targeted traffic from related sites is the major benefit of article marketing.

Successful web marketing companies add social sharing buttons to their articles posted in article directories. The basic purpose of article marketing is to generate interest in the website and it establishes credibility as an expert in the niche. It is very simple to perform the task of article marketing and article marketing does not cost any money. The niche/category will determine the types of articles an individual or business organization will write. Article marketing is a vital component of web marketing strategy and it inspires internet users interested in a specific product.

The title of the article should be carefully selected and it improves Search Engine Optimization (SEO). The article title should be short, concise, and SEO friendly and keywords should be placed at the beginning of article title. Article marketing will become effective only if the articles published are of high quality and there are fewer chances of low quality articles attract attention. It is an excellent practice to share articles on social media sites like Facebook, Twitter, Instagram and Pinterest. Ezine Articles, Squidoo, Article Alley, Hub Pages, Go Articles, Articles Base, and iSnare are the best article directories. An article directory website is rated in terms of quality content, ease of use as well as potential reach.

Increased sales, shorter sales cycles, strong customer loyalty and cost efficiency are the prized features of article marketing. Blog posts, video blogs, animation, live action video shoots, Infographics, long form guides, white papers, ebooks, web copy, product descriptions and press releases are the most popular content types of today. It is to be ensured that article marketing initiatives of a company are scaled up to the needs of company. Every business owner can benefit from article marketing and article marketing is an excellent tool to build business. The article marketing provides valuable knowledge and it helps to build credibility in business.

Prominent article directories have a very broad reach and it helps businesses to reach more customers and potential customers. Article marketing can be used as an excellent method to drive traffic to a specific website and it plays a key role in promoting products and services of a website. The article marketing will give new customers to a business and it can be effectively used as a marketing tool. 99% of article directories are free to use and few of the article directories use upgrade feature. Article marketing can be used to attract, engage and delight customers of the contemporary digital era.

Article marketing is one of the most powerful, effective, and useful web marketing strategies of today. The article marketing campaign of today drives conversions and it eventually pays off well in the end. Quality content should be produced consistently to improve site traffic and article marketing engages target buyers. Brand awareness is one of the prime benefits of article marketing and article marketing can also be used to educate customers. Article marketing helps a business to build trust with target audience and good content is helpful in fostering strong customer relationships.

Businesses of today need to provide value to customers by providing quality, engaging, fresh and unique content. It is a well known fact that valuable content helps a business organization to build authority as well as credibility. Content can be used to position the business as an industry expert and an ideal article engages the consumer in every stage of the buying process. Article marketing is used to engage, entertain and educate customers as well as prospective customers. The article marketing is an incredibly easy promotional method and article marketing combined with content marketing produces outstanding results. The writing aspect of article marketing can be outsourced to professional writers and article marketing plays a huge role in the success of a business.

THANK YOU!

If you enjoyed this book or benefitted from it anyway, then I would like to ask you for a favour: would you be kind enough to leave a review for this book on Amazon.com? It would be greatly appreciated.

Other Books by MAHINROOP PM

Mega Book of Website Designing

Blogging Masterclass Package 2018

Big Book of Vatakara